arreboles

arrebol

(l. *rubore*) *m.* Color rojo de las nubes heridas
por los rayos del sol. *Vox Diccionario general
ilustrado de la lengua española* (Bibliograf, S. A., 1985)

Reddish hue of clouds penetrated by the sun's rays.

BOYER RICKEL

arreboles

Wesleyan University Press

Published by University Press of New England
Hanover and London

Wesleyan University Press
Published by University Press of New England,
Hanover, NH 03755
© 1991 by Boyer Rickel
All rights reserved
Printed in the United States of
America   5 4 3 2 1
CIP data appear at the end of the book

Some of the poems in this book appeared
originally in *The Antioch Review, Carolina
Quarterly, crazyhorse, Hayden's Ferry Review,
Ironwood, The North American Review, North
Dakota Quarterly, The Ohio Review, On Tap,
OUT/LOOK, Prairie Schooner, Puerto del Sol, The
Sonora Review, Telescope, The Yale Review.*
"Elegy" and "From Where It's Dark" appeared in
Poetry.

I'd like to thank Julie Willson, Karen Brennan, and
Barbara Cully for their help in the making of
many of these poems, and especially Steve Orlen,
whose faith time and again steadied my steps.

For Gary Kautto

Contents

Education of the Poet

I must have been four, our California summer,
a broken tamarisk in our sandy backyard the site
of many mysteries—diarrhea of a hobo
dribbled at its foot, the foot of a gopher
chewed off in a trap my father set, who grew ill
at sight of this work of his hands,
hands that at the piano keyboard played
the same Bach four-note phrase a hundred
times to hear the possibilities.

I heard beneath the tamarisk my brother's
explanations. "Prevent," he said, "means
to start something, to begin it," in answer
to my question about Smokey the Bear:
"Only *you* can prevent forest fires!"
Only *you* can start forest fires, I said
to myself, over and over, head
down, adjusting to the weight—this
was a world of responsibility.

These were the days when buffalo heads and Mercurys
could still be found in dime-store change,
and steel pennies from World War II,
blackened as if charred by war's fires.
Our cardboard coin albums with punched-out circles
seemed valuable according to their weights—
as pages filled the albums grew heavier,
difficult for me to handle, reaching on my toes
to slide them from the bookcase shelf.

Home from shopping trips, we raced
to see who could empty Dad's trouser pockets,
who could squeeze open Mom's green
football-shaped coin purse first, matching coins
with their values in the red collector's book,
a book with new words like "mint-condition," "uncirculated,"
and "priceless," which, as my brother explained,
meant a thing was of so little value it was worthless.
If I found one, I should simply hand it over to him.

for my brother, Richard

The Lover

Near the yard's back gate
where the wild sunflowers have blackened, the eucalyptus leaves
reddened with winter cold,

my friend is planting a golden
barrel cactus given him by a neighbor boy.
Forty soon, he appears

years younger, the green
shivers of light in his eyes and his child's grin—
he loves the cool mud

that coats his fingers, that he rubs
on his jeans as he stands, admiring his work. His smile
is aimless, for nothing, unless

himself. The first night
we talked seriously, it was winter. We sat
before a fire that threw

red and yellow slivers
across our shirts and faces, the whole room—
empty except his easel

at the center and two stools
we drew to the fire's edge—rocked by the flickering.
And he, then only

thirty-four, grinned in
at the flames, poking chunks of mesquite into place with
the ease and certainty

of one who makes things
with his hands. No, he said, he was not ready yet
to care for anyone.

As I watched this man,
abstract, more the task he undertook than himself,
I felt as if something, the very

Devil, perhaps, had slipped
a cold and lucky coin into my palm.
So I held on.

Elegy

Clayton Rickel, April 19–August 11, 1984

1

The town all day awaited a storm.
My sister made a sound; my mother took her arm.
The rain fell lightly when it fell.

My brother's wife wore heels that dug into the soil,
and a cloud the shape of shoulder blades settled on the hill.
Sometimes I can't remember how to use a chair.

My wide-eyed aunt rocked lightly on her toes.
My father lost his way and found his way again.
My brother turned a mirror toward the wall.

The rabbi sang a song; I couldn't hear the words.
The shadow of a bird hugged the hillside lawn.
My mother said she felt my nephew near.

2

Who decides how time is measured?
Would you say a baby's wild or tame?

Are there ghosts? Is this a test?
Who decides who gets the most?

Am I alone? Is fear appropriate?
Who decides when to kneel or when to sit?

I think the rain disturbs my brother's wife.
I'll stand off to the side.

What's at the end of what we cannot know?
What's in the middle of the road?

Who decides what can't be willed, or bought, or where we go?
Which detail will we all forget?

Two Childhood Songs

Our fathers had nicknames
and our mothers were sedentary

and our fathers' friends
were familiar and legendary

and our mothers' friends scented.
I hid behind the couch on which they sat

like six packages of matches, trim
and potent, conversation throbbing—

of *Huck Finn* and McCarthyism.
The moon rose; I was sent to bed.

All across the continent,
the color of fear was red.

*

My brother was a pencil.
Eight years old, he dove

into a creek and came up lame.
America had polio.

Nurses fed him pills,
kin filled our home, and

I hardly noticed he was gone.
America was in a boom.

One leg shrank; he grew warm.
My brother's friend was President.

I hardly knew I'd been born.
The world was one block long.

Alexandrian

March 1904
4 A.M. Shadows in the wrinkled bedsheets.
A green vase on the bookshelf
wrapped in bands of light
through the blinds.

Then the tiny whoosh and crack
of paper landing on its edge—the fallen sketch
of a naked boy suggests
Cavafy has failed to understand

a man's love
for a man.
He thinks he does.

At 5 A.M. he tacks the drawing up again,
and wanders room to room
making sure he is alone.

*

1933
He had bought it years before, in a hurry,
on his way to Cairo for pleasure.
"Then," he added, "I was young and strong,
and not ugly." (Of course, these things

he wrote down, because the tumor
had him by the throat.) Now the worn
leather suitcase lay open, filled
with items for the hospital. Where

in one final motion—it was something
like a man, though seen
from very far away, surrounded by a wall—

he drew a circle
on a blank sheet of paper
and placed a period in the center.

From Where It's Dark

1

I stood outside the window
of a lighted house
and saw a boy rear up
from a kitchen table;
his mother, passing by,
turned to test the effect
of a certain arch to her brow.

All faces alike enough,
two eyes, a nose, a mouth—
a stranger's features
barely seen behind their own—
they went about their business
wondering what
brought on the changes.

2

Monty Clift, his face all light
until a car crash froze the left side shut.
"I was lovely," he wrote his brother,
"I can safely say
there was not one characteristic
of my face remaining."

The Civil War, *Raintree County*—
they recomposed his face and waited.
And though the camera mostly caught him
from a distance, or closer in,
off to his better side,
there was a new war waged
no skill in lighting could disguise.

3
In this dream my young friend is sad.
I know what he's thinking. He's followed me
from the empty hotel bar
where a jukebox
serenades
to a sidewalk table cluttered
with cups.
If I haven't acknowledged him yet beside me,
it's because the dreamer
doesn't wish to share his thoughts
with the dreamed.   Silver lights
strung along the awning
starken the pale skin of my friend
and whiten my hair and mustache.
I am almost an old man.
If I haven't acknowledged him yet,
it's because the dreamer
enjoys a story most
when witnessed
as though by someone else.

4
Inside a lighted room, the window
blackened, I play the game
of staring eye to eye

at my reflection;
the fleshy parts
begin to drift—my cheeks, chin, forehead,

separating continents.
What I am, trapped
in darkness, is flesh

which falls away.
This is what I think I mean
to say in affirmation

of light which is
a love of change and nearly
all we have to go by.

for Gail Orlen

Exposure

What the hare upright in the weeds felt last,
the attitude of the ears—the wind froze them
into place, flat against the head—the legs
hunched tight in back and raised unevenly
in front as though ready for a spring or
warding off a blow . . . not an ounce of resignation!
But if the hare is taken from the weeds
and placed on its side in the snow, how much
like someone sleeping it becomes, wrapped
into itself, the front paws actively dreaming.

We call talk of weather "small talk," and
at the drugstore exchange some with the clerk
as we sort change for the Sunday paper.
But have you noticed how the drunk, his face
purpled by years of exposure, having begged
enough for his paper, passes over it,
speaking quickly and too loud about his life
in Colorado, the odd jobs and friends, how good
the hunting, how good the price of everything.

Wasps

          among the flickering
cottonwood leaves, the tree fort
all splintery scrap, cardboard
barely tacked,
and the earth miles below
for the nine-year-old me,
such dread I felt
in the distance
between the steady limbs up here
in the air
and the water down there
of the canal, roiling brown.

Airborne, wasps
are limitless and lethal, I thought,
and better than thinking
felt the tug
of flight, inhaling
the sweet smell of cardboard rot,
the high sweet smell
of sweat-stained
socks and underwear
on the tree fort floor,
momentary attractant
to a six-wasp squadron, hovering,

though I am troubled
and I am thrilled
by this gentle
stroking of a new best friend,
the whole world
humming and sweetly heavy
all the way home (how
did I make it
those miles down?)
and through dinner
and into bed that night
and the nights that follow.

The Exposure of Form

As my father played
the concluding fugue,
each sure note

released a weight
from my adolescent heart.
I passed among

the well-wishing crowd
as though untouched, imagining
perfection

in remaining so,
imagining Beethoven's
loss—how it

drew him inward
to greatness—
and shook my father's hand.

*

My friend jumped again and again
from the limb of a cottonwood, naked,
drunk and careless, the river high.

Cars angling the park road
threw light on the branches; I saw him
midair and raving in the headlights' glare.

On the muddy bank a hundred yards downstream,
he said the light blinded him, and he gave in
to the current, drifting a while, seeing what was there

when he was not. I will always remember the ease
of his smile as he confessed this giving in.
We hugged each other for a moment, challenging Beethoven.

II

Night-Singing

Not the thought an eyeblink can decide . . .
Not the depthlessness
as you sit in the yard at night

staring at the blackness
around the stars—
a body hurled into space might never stop.

If something small . . . small, at the center like a flower—
if something felt could take the shape of lupine, or foxglove,
and be Flower and not a flower.

Late one night, a bird song stopped me.
I was just out walking.
I felt lucky—it sounded like a secret, a song

a child might hum
measuring his uniqueness—until I remembered
the mockingbird's uncommon habit.

Coolness along an edge,
as though a knife blade might rest
an hour on a wrist . . .

Love's a gap into which hate also precisely fits.
Love shakes a leg and sits.
Love knows the sun will burn five billion years, then blow the galaxy to bits.

Two Mothers in The Cloisters

One eye half-covered by the lid, the other open to the world,
the cracked, five-hundred-year-old Madonna,
a headless baby in her arms, smiled

while the other mother, gray
and gap-toothed, talked about her crazy son
to anyone who'd listen.

Her voice broke off, and I could see
the Madonna had no feet,
and the guide-ropes were covered in sky-blue velvet.
The living mother's eyes
never fell on objects, but searched the open spaces . . .

On dreams there's no consensus.
Half the day I walked around sick from a dream
as though I'd swallowed a toxic substance.
For centuries people thought of them as omens.
Now we're told we *are* what we create—
I *am* my loved one, her lace-trimmed water-colored skirt . . .

Forbearance. Not the Ancients' notion
of Fate, though I can feel it
in Oedipus's demeanor at the end
as he walks blinded out of Thebes,
or in the grim composure
of the fifteenth-century Madonna. As if to say,

Since we can't will the knowledge we need to live,
we make,
and when the thing is done,
acknowledge its beauty and its brokenness:

I dreamed I carved up my mother with a hunting knife.

The mother with a mad son smiled past my face.

On Father's Day

We took a long walk, up and up, around a mountain.
Across our path, a red-and-yellow bird
jumped pine to aspen. A vein stood
purpling on my father's brow.
                              The wind picked up,
the crackling, sun-dried needles scattered, the forest groaned.
My father buttoned his tan and spotless coat.
He placed a small pink tablet under his tongue.

Twice I've watched friends' fathers die and seen
how death makes boys of men; shrunken, little more
than kindling lost among the sheets,
they must be fed and dressed and reminded
of their names.

So when my father stumbled, falling backward
through a bed of ferns,
I was familiar with the hollow limbs
hanging at my sides—the sudden
panic that makes a blank of all the dailiness.
And then my father laughed; I was in the world again; he took my hand.

Once my father's mother said, to calm me in a storm,
"Tell a secret to make the wind die down."
I thought the storm would never end because I couldn't think of one.
Of course, I was wrong.
Like a feather rocking in still air, my father
made it down the mountainside, easy. I thought,
Only one thing in this world never ends. And I was wrong again.

Almost Breathing

Hector was some mama's
big dumb baby too and Lincoln
and Lauren Bacall
and each in his or her own way
had a chance to bounce
the world
around a bit,
passing off a momentary
style of voice
or actually
doing things—heroes
do things.
Even if it's just a whistle
the rest of us
hear it

and whistle a little
to ourselves.
Like the horizon I see
walking this winter morning
along the Charles
(the mirrored 60-story
Hancock building
and row on row
of stolid
brownstones),
each generation has
its own interpretation:
in a whistle
one hears a column of stomping
freshly

polished boots,
and the next
a call to ravening
sex.
Take me, for example,
out walking, the little
cloud puffs
of my breath inspiring
an idea: if I whistle,
a white
line of steam will mark
the melody.
No such luck.
Somehow whistling doesn't do it
whereas breathing is enough.

for Jim Weeks

Wait

March winds brought dust—the orange trees, cypresses,
candy wrappers blown
down the gutters, all things
on this side of the ground

lightly coated, as though faded,
in training for what the sun will do all summer long
in Tucson.
        A man I can imagine a lifetime with
has put aside his paints and stored
one last half-finished canvas—unfocused shape,
a many-tailed cat or palm branch.
                The wings beneath his eyes
withdraw, the lines release
their hold; a drink, then a double, the skin inflates.
When he can't feel, he says he waits.

Not young enough to know his own heart well, he asks
that I don't question him.

That we are walking down a public street
where strangers' faces harden when I take his hand
is not what makes me drop a little off the pace.

I think of rooms, blinds drawn—red tile, Indian
geometric rugs—holding color for generations, protected from the light;

and light itself, the daily dying out, the sunset blur
of lawn and concrete walk;
              how some things
come alive, my two gray cats at dusk: stretching,
muscles ripple—a final shake, they dart into the evening,

and once they hit the street, disappear, as if into a lake.

The Bloated Goldfish

       in the tank behind the bar used to start
every time a drink hit the counter. You'd think
it would have gotten used to it. Now it just floats
and a woman two stools from me stares at it
like she could will the thing to move again.
Or maybe she's like me and knows if she turns
her head, some motion just out of sight will
fool her into thinking the thing still lives—
she'll get off her stool and punch the numbers
of a familiar song on the jukebox, or simply
walk out. Instead, she stares, making sure.
And I watch her, a woman I've seen a hundred times
in this bar, and like all the times before,
I don't say a word. You never get used to it.

for Mike Hendershot

Summer Elegy

George Rickel, 1887–1965

August morning, dog days' end, a last blue river overhead
snaking westward where our weather comes from—
low gray clouds close in over heat-drugged Tucson.

Cypresses outside my door are bent, dazed by the threat
or merely skeptical—live things grow noncommittal
in the desert; I see neighbors watering lawns
on my way to buy the morning paper.

Last July, one downpour washed out houses built
too near a ravine—a bubbling river where moments before
a dry arroyo lay—
                    palo verde branches, shoes
and Coleman coolers, bobbing in the front-page photographs;
a broken line marked the path the woman's body took,
torn from the porch that overlooked the wash.

Today, after hours of thickening clouds, sheets of rain sweep over town.
Sirens—I hear them from my living room—race aid in all directions.

Often after summer storms, my father's father
would walk along the residential streets to smell
wet creosote and sidewalks being swept.
                            Stooped, leathered
by the sun (I thought of him as what's left standing
when lightning strikes a tree), he'd fold my fingers
into his papery hand, and show me how things
blurred for months by relentless heat
become distinct—the suddenly rational palms and sky-

reflecting puddles. He taught me to love such clarity,
and said it was a lie. "The rains are good but the land's
no good at taking them in."

        Distrusting God, he hardly slept
his last few months. "What I can't see," he said,
"I spend the nights imagining."

After the storm, I look out from my covered porch, the atmosphere
so clarified, I see zigzagging lines—children's
voices and birdcalls, visible—in the air.

        My father's father waits
beside the ornamental orange tree by the gate.

         Turn from kin
and you'll go spinning till the end. So I step down.
Two grown men, we walk the quiet streets, hand in hand.

Our Names

This morning, finches picking at saltbush seed
startled at the motion of a trowel
as I did at the high
white scream of the deaf boy
next door, shaken from his dreams.

Where was he moments before, I wondered,
that waking should unsettle him so.

So little land, so little yard
for him and all the others
to adventure in
in summer. Five families in shacks

on a lot the size of ours—
just room enough, we calculate,
for two grown men, a garden, and cat
to discover together
their individual selves.

This evening, sipping drinks
on the porch, the cicada
buzz and heat and alcohol
so intermixed
we are an endless
coil of sound,

we almost fail to hear our names—
the next-door children,
walking along the railing of the fence,
climb the chinaberry tree

and now they're
on a roof. The deaf boy,
trailing a cape,
is standing on the very
ridge, whistling as he waves.

Downpour

The garden, lush with poppies, anemones, reds
on blues on yellows, is,
during this, the first hard storm in months,
a marketplace, spatulate
leaves and wind-tossed buds

a bartering, purposeful throng.
And the man who tends it, who just stepped out,
who stands on moony nights or even
in this daylight downpour, slack
as if listening

for the need of growing things,
this man, if you could see him as I do
from the kitchen door
in secret, like a cat,
is love in flesh and bone

for all his giving,
the almost-glow imparted
to the iris blade he runs
like living ribbon through his fingers—
is emptiness, the one

beside me here this afternoon
and mornings as I roll my pant legs up
to wade the low
cool household lake
between his dreams and mine.

The Watchers

Around midnight, a full October moon,
the sky not deep but flat and low and black, and six clouds
fully lit, white without disappointment, with visible depth;

the kind of night, my friend Michael says, when the small planet's light
warms your skin, yet the dry fall air gets under it—he shivers.

As we drive, blue green white neon signs burn cool, independent
of us, the way our dreams sometimes are—
the bleating lamb's head floating in the air, or hubcap
someone skimmed along the lake top.

In this light we drive the length of Tucson's longest boulevard
out of town, and blurt our random daily disappointments:

Moon above the Rincons,
what do you care for Mike's wife, who is probably sad tonight;
or the letter I put off writing
to a favorite aunt whose husband died.

High above Tucson, the ground, our skin, the leaves
of desert shrubs, plated silver by the moon; in the valley,
city streetlights stitching in every direction.

Nights like these are outside time, Mike says,
like family photos you've known so well, you were there

until your mother told you in your twenty-fifth year
you weren't yet born.

In one snapshot, the split, hand-set, horizontal fence logs;
the banked white snow, stretching to the farmhouse and beyond;
smoke curling from the chimney so familiar

that in his favorite flannel shirt Mike carries its smell—

all this from a time when he was just a vague idea, a pill
of thought, the outcome of one night's unexpected swell
in his father's Air Force uniform—Mike smiles to recall his mother's

enthusiastic voice and side-turned blushing face.
He still sees his father's bomber jacket, the pleated
khaki pants and calf-length coat with golden buttons—*I see them*—

because Mike *was* there and *is*, none of this is speculation.
The moon will slip behind the mountains,
the sun will rise and warm the air and Michael and I

will not be, and always will be there, and here.

III

Taormina

At first one imagines von Gloeden
   in complete control.
On beaches, on palazzo steps
   and patios
the naked youths he photographed
   compliant,
some blank, some staring
   coolly back, told
how to stand, how to let
   the penis hang.
Aroused a little, he may have hidden
   an extra moment
behind the camera curtain.

        The modern traveler, like Wilde
           or Gide
        eighty years before, who walks
           the ocean side
        and streets, who hopes to glimpse
           the pink and olive
        flawless skin of youths, not
           in sepia
        as in the prints, but alive,
           will discover
        the Hellenic ideal wears
           designer jeans
        and bobs to unknown tunes,
           a Walkman
        plugged into his ears.

And then you see a small
   nude boy
who holds, shoulder-high,
   the way he might
during "show-and-tell," a fish,
   large and pale,
overexposed, like a ghost;
   a boy who stares
wide-eyed at you, not wholly
   innocent, yet
discomposed, not comprehending
   why he pokes
a finger in the fish's mouth.
   At this, deep
in the groin a tide sweeps out;
   and reason lies
abandoned on the shore to rot.

for Roger Bowen

Night Sweats

Bill Tynes, 1956–1987

In Placentia,
nine eucalyptus limbs
appear to bicker,
pushed erratic
by a midnight breeze.

The window rattles.
He tries to see
a pattern—nine
lightning strokes,
nine branching paths to

one phone ringing
on the stage of
Broadway's darkened
New Amsterdam Theatre.

*

           Mindless, pulling
           weeds this afternoon,
           I push my fingers
           through the warm
           dirt crust and am

           stunned by the
           cold wetness
           underground. It's
           such a small
           discovery, like

                              a shadow or
                              a question that,
                              once it's posed,
                              won't go away.

                    *

Outside the fence,
a winter breeze
climbs a tamarisk
and drops
into the yard.

And treads the gleaming
back-porch steps
without a sound
and finds the bedroom
door ajar.

And wraps itself,
as cool and smooth
as sheets in December,
around a trembling head.

Night Sweats 2

Two men lie folded in sleep,

        a blue sheet draped over their bodies.

One, awakening to the other's sweat,

        slips out to get the damp cloth they keep

refrigerated for nights like this.

        If the other wakes, he'll weep and shake.

So the one does the best he can to gentle him

        through the delirium and back into dream.

Tonight the other tries something different.

        He holds his breath, releasing the air

so gradually, he finds he can almost keep

        the shaking away. He lies so still

in the arms of the one he loves

        that the one who loves him imagines

for an instant as he drifts into sleep

        that the other no longer breathes.

for Michael Canter

The Grief of Achilles

In their dreams, the warriors
left the temporary tented pavilions,
disregarding the armor, the shields

and proud horses won in battle.
They set sail for home, dreaming
the sounds of home, with no great care

for the sound of *kydos*.
But there was one among them
who couldn't sleep, Patroclus,

who walked at dawn along the shore
envisioning the abandoned
breaking waters: the ships gone,

the pavilions in tatters—a collective
longing had swept them away. One
who found himself so alone,

he discovered the destiny
of another. The power in his heart
withdrew the wind; the fleet

of a people paused at sea
on the edge of waking—
he borrowed the hero's

shield and sword and immortal horses.
To wear another man's armor,
is that what love is?

And in your case, Patroclus,
in wearing Achilles',
to drive him out to his glory

and to his destruction,
dragging a civilization with him,
beginning countless others.

"Winterreise"

Schubert walked a path, a song
  he sang, not morbidly
or in fear, but in contrast
  to what might come,
to what would not,
  in his voice a gladness.
I hear this song in the spastic

blind wriggling of worms
  that eat the agave root,
the agave's outer blades
  shrinking inward,
yellow, unable to stand.
  And in the gap between
the dog's god-powerful nose

and the cat's flattened ears,
  each animal poised
at the absolute limit, one
  angstrom unit beyond which
they'd wrap themselves,
  fang and claw, into
a nuclear cloud of hair. There's

a color that is many colors—
  in Spanish, a word that sings,
arreboles. This color you see
  in clouds on the horizon
opposite the setting sun.
  Not the fires that bring tears,
but the color that moves

opposite these brilliances,
   akin to mauve and rose and violet.
Like musical overtones—strike
   the piano's middle C
and hunch down close
   to the spray of strings,
down by the sounding board.

Listen: the Others, not God,
   but something nameless,
like ghosts or angels,
   more felt than seen or heard.
The hope that hovers, pure,
   above the written,
the drawn, the legislated plan.

"Spring Sonata"

Robert O'Conner, 1896–1986

The high-backed chair in which the maestro sits
is covered in tapestry of flowers and hunting hounds.
Today he's ninety. Red silk robe sleeves fall,
almost empty, to either side of his limbs.
One by one he greets the guests by name and
holds their hands in both of his. And then a hush.
Two old men, his students once, will play,

at his request, a sonata Allegro for violin.
But at its end they begin the Adagio, the maestro
twisting in mild surprise—he's tired—or anger.
And then the Scherzo, whereupon he curses
and pounds his cane, a nurse rushing in to
take him by the arm, as his students play on,
and walk him down the hall and into bed.

At the Funeral

1
My father, humpbacked and bent, forms
                                    a human question mark

as he shuffles across the green,
                        clean-cropped cemetery lawn

with help of a cane.
                    As if simply taking his hand

will resolve my gladness
                        and pain at the sight of him,

I quicken my step
                too late to reach him, absorbed in a swirl

of in-laws and in-laws' friends
                        at the edge of the grave.

2
The rabbi sings, and a tall,
                        grim-faced man—

has he read my mind?—
                    leans to explain: "The small

black strip of cloth
                close relatives wear

represents the rending
                    of mourners' clothes.

What's left of a ritual
                    of grief. In centuries past,

they'd sit for a week
                    on a rough wooden bench.''

3
My brother's house is
                    a house of voices, twenty people

talking all at once. Surely
                    that is Audrey (the woman

we just buried, mother
                    of my brother's wife) complaining

of the heat; and that the voice
                    of Leah (my niece, 3,

a mile away at school) asking
                    her ''Bobe,'' Audrey, whose

eyes fill with light,
                    for a glass of ice.

Poem to Begin the Second Decade of AIDS

The dog, alive, Lucy, my light, sleeps
   on the couch I'd have trained her off of
had not someone coaxed her, repeatedly,
   to clamber up, then lie down along
his outstretched legs; Gary, alive, who,

   had he had his way at first, wouldn't
have let her live with us at all for fear
   she'd dig up the bulbs and seedlings,
or strip the bark from young acacias
   and mesquites in our yard alive with

four years of his ceaseless shovel, shoulder,
   rake and sweat. The hour darkens, sweetens,
whenever I ask how long for all of this—
   November lettuces, April poppies, Lucy's
dog-fragrant, humid *hrumph* across my

   rising/falling, almost-sleeping chest,
how long the *chauk, chauk* of Gary's spade,
   the swells and waves of caliche and dust.
This poem is far too private for anybody
   but us. This poem will make certain

close friends blush, who prefer poems be
   like linens they can put in drawers,
sure of their place and use. Today I
   thought of this as I took up our blue
wool blanket, a week-long winter freeze

having passed, folding once, twice,
a cloudless, geometrically diminishing sky;
then twice again, all compact, tangible
potential, ready to unfold and warm or
simply drape across a reclining form.

January 1990

Notes

"Alexandrian." The second part of this poem is derived from details in Robert Liddell's *Cavafy: A Critical Biography* and the "Biographical Notes" in Edmund Keeley and Philip Sherrard's *C. P. Cavafy: Complete Poems.*

"Two Mothers in The Cloisters." A branch of the Metropolitan Museum of Art, The Cloisters is located in Fort Tryon Park, overlooking the Hudson River, in New York City. Incorporating architectural features of several European cloisters, it houses an important collection of medieval art.

"Taormina." Baron Wilhelm von Gloeden (1856–1931) moved from his native Germany sometime in the late 1870s to Taormina, Sicily, where he established himself as a professional photographer with a particular interest in the male nude. His work was considered pornographic by the Italian Fascist government, which seized his glass photographic plates in 1936.

" 'Winterreise.' " Franz Schubert's song cycle "Winterreise" ("A Winter's Journey"), based on twenty-four poems by German Romantic poet Wilhelm Müller, was completed five months before Schubert's death in 1828. He was thirty-one.

" 'Spring Sonata.' " Early listeners of Ludwig van Beethoven's Sonata for Violin and Piano No. 5 in F Major, Op. 24, renamed the work "Spring Sonata," responding to what they considered its light, spirited quality.

University Press of New England publishes books under its own imprint and is the publisher for Brandeis University Press, Brown University Press, Clark University Press, University of Connecticut, Dartmouth College, Middlebury College Press, University of New Hampshire, University of Rhode Island, Tufts University, University of Vermont, and Wesleyan University Press.

Boyer Rickel teaches poetry and nonfiction workshops at the University of Arizona in Tucson. "I grew up in a household of music, a household of teaching," he says of his childhood in Tempe, Arizona, where his parents taught music. This background resulted in an awareness of the music in language and an emphasis on "ear training" for his writing students. He graduated with a B.A. in English from Oberlin College and an M.F.A. in poetry from the University of Arizona. His poetry has appeared in such publications as *Antioch Review, Field, Poetry, Iowa Review,* and *Yale Review.* He is the recipient of a Tucson/Pima Arts Council Literary Award and a grant from the Arizona Commission on the Arts.

This book was designed by Sally Harris/Summer Hill Books, Weathersfield, Vermont, and set in Aldus type by Brevis Press, Bethany, Connecticut.

Library of Congress Cataloging-in-Publication Data

Rickel, Boyer.
  Arreboles / by Boyer Rickel.
    p. cm. — (Wesleyan new poets)
  Includes bibliographical references.
  ISBN 0–8195–2197–3 (cl). — ISBN 0–8195–1199–4 (pa)
  I. Title. II. Series.
PS3568.I35335A89 1991
811'.54—dc20   91–7634